Keep this pocket-si͟ you are visiting Pres͟ the locality.

Whether you are in your car or on foot, you will enjoy an evocative journey back in time. Compare the Preston of old with what you can see today— see how the streets of the town and its parks and open spaces have changed; examine the shops and buildings and notice how they have been altered or replaced; look at fine details such as lamp-posts, shop fascias and trade signs; and see the many alterations to Preston and its surrounding area that have taken place unnoticed during our lives, some of which we may have taken for granted.

At the turn of a page you will gain fascinating insights into Preston's unique history.

FRANCIS FRITH'S
pocket ALBUM

PRESTON

A POCKET ALBUM

Adapted from an original book by
CLIFF HAYES

First published in the United Kingdom in 2005 by
Frith Book Company Ltd

ISBN 1-85937-945-1
Text and Design copyright © Frith Book Company Ltd
Photographs copyright © The Francis Frith Collection

The Frith photographs and the Frith logo are reproduced under licence from Heritage
Photographic Resources Ltd, the owners of the Frith archive and trademarks

British Library Cataloguing in Publication Data

Preston - A Pocket Album
Adapted from an original book by Cliff Hayes

Frith Book Company Ltd
Frith's Barn, Teffont,
Salisbury, Wiltshire SP3 5QP
Tel: +44 (0) 1722 716 376
Email: info@francisfrith.co.uk
www.francisfrith.co.uk

Printed and bound in Great Britain by MPG, Bodmin

Front Cover: **PRESTON, FISHERGATE** 1929 / 82676T
The colour-tinting is for illustrative purposes only, and is not intended to be historically accurate.

Frontispiece: **PRESTON, FISHERGATE** C1955 / P113009

AS WITH ANY HISTORICAL DATABASE THE FRITH ARCHIVE IS CONSTANTLY
BEING CORRECTED AND IMPROVED AND THE PUBLISHERS WOULD WELCOME
INFORMATION ON OMISSIONS OR INACCURACIES

FISHERGATE 1903 / 50065

CONTENTS

FRANCIS FRITH
VICTORIAN PIONEER

Francis Frith, founder of the world-famous photographic archive, was a complex and multi-talented man. A devout Quaker and a highly successful Victorian businessman, he was philosophic by nature and pioneering in outlook. By 1855 he had already established a wholesale grocery business in Liverpool, and sold it for the astonishing sum of £200,000, which is the equivalent today of over £15,000,000. Now in his thirties, and captivated by the new science of photography, Frith set out on a series of pioneering journeys up the Nile and to the Near East.

INTRIGUE AND EXPLORATION

He was the first photographer to venture beyond the sixth cataract of the Nile. Africa was still the mysterious 'Dark Continent', and Stanley and Livingstone's historic meeting was a decade into the future. The conditions for picture taking confound belief. He laboured for hours in his wicker dark-room in the sweltering heat of the desert, while the volatile chemicals fizzed dangerously in their trays. Back in London he exhibited his photographs and was 'rapturously cheered' by members of the Royal Society. His reputation as a photographer was made overnight.

VENTURE OF A LIFE-TIME

By the 1870s the railways had threaded their way across the country, and Bank Holidays and half-day Saturdays had been made obligatory by Act of Parliament. All of a sudden the working man and his family were able to enjoy days out, take holidays, and see a little more of the world.

With typical business acumen, Francis Frith foresaw that these new tourists would enjoy having souvenirs to commemorate their days out. For the next thirty years he travelled the country by train and by pony and trap, producing fine photographs of seaside resorts and beauty spots that were keenly bought by millions of Victorians. These prints were painstakingly pasted into family albums and pored over during the dark nights of winter, rekindling precious memories of summer excursions. Frith's studio was soon supplying retail shops all over the country, and by 1890 F Frith & Co had become the greatest specialist photographic publishing company in the world, with over 2,000 sales outlets, and pioneered the picture postcard.

FRANCIS FRITH'S LEGACY

Francis Frith had died in 1898 at his villa in Cannes, his great project still growing. The archive he created continued in business for another seventy years. By 1970 it contained over a third of a million pictures showing 7,000 British towns and villages.

Frith's legacy to us today is of immense significance and value, for the magnificent archive of evocative photographs he created provides a unique record of change in the cities, towns and villages throughout Britain over a century and more. Frith and his fellow studio photographers revisited locations many times down the years to update their views, compiling for us an enthralling and colourful pageant of British life and character.

We are fortunate that Frith was dedicated to recording the minutiae of everyday life. For it is this sheer wealth of visual data, the painstaking chronicle of changes in dress, transport, street layouts, buildings, housing, engineering and landscape that captivates us so much today, offering us a powerful link with the past and with the lives of our ancestors.

Computers have now made it possible for Frith's many thousands of images to be accessed almost instantly. The archive offers every one of us an opportunity to examine the places where we and our families have lived and worked down the years. Its images, depicting our shared past, are now bringing pleasure and enlightenment to millions around the world a century and more after his death.

FISHERGATE C1955 / P113026

PROUD PRESTON
AN INTRODUCTION

THE ROMANS do not appear to have occupied the area that is Preston. Roman coins and bits of pottery have been found around Preston, but it was out at Ribchester and Walton that they had their forts. One theory is that the River Ribble ran much deeper and faster in Roman times, and fording the river at this point would have been too dangerous.

Tradition states that Athelstan, King of the Mercians and West Saxons, the grandson of Alfred the Great, passed through Preston capturing all before him on his way to beat the Danish invaders in Northumberland. The monks from Ripon, who accompanied him, prayed for his soul, and for strength to conquer the enemy. For this they were granted the town of Preston. Later, the town was transferred to the ownership of the Archbishop of York, which seems hard to believe now. During the Danish invasions of York, Yorkshire lost its grip on the town, and Harold II's brother Tosti was given Preston as an income.

After the Norman conquest, the town, along with much of the area of the Ribble Valley, passed to Roger de Poitou, one of the great Norman barons and friend of William the Conqueror. In 1339, after Lancaster backed the wrong side in one of the power struggles of the time, Edward III took Preston under royal protection, and it was then that a municipal form of rule was established.

Preston was the principal town in the Hundred of Amounderness. Because Preston is so ideally situated, it has always figured large in the plans of people travelling north or south to and from Scotland. It is half-way up Lancashire, so this position made it an ideal compromise between the old seat of government, Lancaster, and the emerging power-houses of industry and commerce in the north-west, most notably in Warrington, Manchester and the surrounding towns. Preston is roughly half-way between London and Glasgow, so early travellers

had to make a stop here. It was always a thorn in Preston's side that some of its early visitors came expecting the refinements of the larger cities, and did not leave with the right impression of the town.

The name Preston means 'the fortified enclosed place of priests'. Many say St Wilfrid was the first to mention the town in writing in 1086 as Prestone. In 1094 it was spelt as it is now, but by 1179-80 it was Presteton or de Prestona. From then on it has stayed more or less as it is today, but we do find Prestun and Prestona in old documents.

Preston was a supporter of the Jacobite cause and the Roman Catholic movement, which in turn was supported by the older Lancashire families. When James VI of Scotland became James I of England, he stayed a few days in Preston on his journey south in 1617. He is said to have had dinner at Hoghton Tower; he liked the loin of beef that he was served so much that he knighted it 'Sir Loin'. In 1323 Robert Bruce descended on Preston and burnt it. The Battle of Preston took place on 17 August 1648, when Oliver Cromwell himself led the Parliamentary army to drive off the Scots/Royalist Army under the Duke of Hamilton. They battled it out on Ribbleton Moor; even though a large part of the Royalists fled south, Cromwell caught them at Wigan and inflicted severe casualties again.

Twice in history a King James III has been proclaimed in the Square at Preston, yet a James III never made it to the throne. In 1715 on November 10, the Earl of Derwentwater and his army were in the Square, paying tribute to James III. Two days later, the Georgian royal forces arrived, and Preston was under siege. More Royalists arrived the next day, and the overwhelming number of troops meant that the siege was soon over. Fifty-eight rebels were hanged at Gallows Hill in the winter that followed. The spot later became the Roman Catholic Church of the English Martyrs, a strange twist of fate – it was the Catholic faith that the rebels were trying to restore. Just thirty years later, almost to the day, Bonnie Prince Charlie was in the Square; he declared his father, The Old Pretender, as James III. He left for

Manchester with Lord Townley and a few volunteers who had joined his 'Scotch Army'. He was soon back and in retreat, and that was the end of the Jacobite Rebellion. Since then, Preston seems to have stayed out of trouble.

Many people feel that Preston should be a city, and it has tried for many years now to attain that status. It has had Parliamentary representation since 1295 or even earlier. The Temperance Movement was put on to a formal footing in Preston, and the word T-Total was first coined here. The first Temperance Hotel opened here, and the first Temperance newspaper was published.

Over the years Preston has always been associated with Guilds, and Guild Processions are held every 20 years: hence the saying 'Every Preston Guild'. The Saxons introduced Guilds into this country. They were formal groups of like-minded individuals linked in trade. The word guild comes from an Anglo-Saxon word, 'gildan', meaning 'to pay'. In fact, the Guild system was not unlike present day insurance schemes. When you were young and strong, you paid in, when you

were working and prosperous, you paid in, and in times of adversity, or when old age made it hard for you, your Guild would look after you and yours. Many a merchant slept easier in his bed knowing that if he did not wake up next morning the Guild would see that he received a decent funeral and that prayers would be said for his soul, and all the rights of burial would be given. The scope of the Guilds changed over the years: they also protected their individual crafts to make sure that standards were maintained and that working practices were fair and just. The first record of a Guild dates from 1328, although permission to form a Guild Merchant is mentioned in Henry II's Charter of c1180.

Between 1328 and 1542 the Guilds paraded the town only infrequently. After that they took place every twenty years for four centuries, with only the 1942 parade being cancelled owing to the War. It was held instead in 1952, ten years later; the next parade was held another twenty years after that in 1972, and the next in 1992, so that the next one is due in the year 2012. But why not restore the dates to their ancient place, 02, 22, 42, and so on? This would give Preston a Millennium Celebration in 2002.

THE ROYAL CHARTERS

Some towns proudly boast of the date they were granted a charter: Preston was granted a charter in about 1179/80 by Henry II. That Charter has since been lost or misplaced, but it is not the only charter Preston was granted. In fact, Preston has been granted 14 charters:

1179 (Missing) King Henry II grants rights to 'Guild Merchants with all the liberties and free customs attached'.

1199 King John confirms the Charter of Henry II.

1227 (Missing) Henry III confirms previous charters.

1252 (Missing) Henry grants land at Fulwood.

1328 (Missing) Edward III confirms all previous charters.

1379 King Richard II confirms previous charters.

1401 King Henry IV confirms previous charters.

1448 King Henry V grants Charter.

1525 King Henry VI grants Charter.

1558 Philip and Mary (some historians say Queen Mary in 1557) confirm previous charters.

1566 Queen Elizabeth grants the 'Great Charter'. This incorporates the names 'Mayor', 'Bailiffs' and 'Burgesses' of the Borough of Preston and grants certain privileges.

1662 Charles II Confirmatory Charter. All offices must swear the Oath of Obedience and Oath of Supremacy.

1685 Charles II confirms the previous charter after the troubles.

1828 George IV orders there be three Coroners, the Mayor, the retiring Mayor and the senior Alderman, and the same three plus the Recorder and all Aldermen shall be ex-officio Justice of the Peace.

Thus there were many charters granted to Preston, and they were well paid for. The Guild Merchants paid the Guild, and the Guild paid the King (or Queen) for the renewal of them.

We are looking up a busy and full Fishergate from the railway station. It is hard to imagine that less than a century before this picture was taken, there was not one business or shop premises to be seen; the whole area of Fishergate consisted of private housing. The names of Preston's Gates (Friargate, Churchgate) comes from 'gata', an Anglo-Saxon word for 'the road to'; thus, Fishergate is 'the way to the fishermen or fishing place', and Friargate is 'the way to the Friary'. The hair cutting saloon and public house on the right of the street mingle with the printer's, draper's and florist's shops.

FISHERGATE

1898 / 40994

13

The gentlemen in their boaters and bowlers and workmen in their flat caps dominate the scene. The town hall tower with its clock rises at the far end of the street. The other tower is that of the Preston Gas Company, and it can just be seen here in the middle of the picture behind the shops. Nearer the camera on the left you can see Burgons Ltd, the grocers, with its striped awning.

FISHERGATE

1903 / 50068

We are standing in Church Street at the spot where it meets Fishergate, with Lancaster Road on the right. On the right we see Miller's Arcade. This fine building was built by the same man who gave the land for Miller's Park. The town hall spire with its large clock face is in the centre, and we can see the old Victorian gents' toilets in the middle of the street with two ornate gas lamps at either end. There was a balcony built into the front of Miller's Arcade so that crowds below could be addressed if the need arose. Hayhurst's Wine Stores is on the corner.

CHURCH STREET

1903 / 50069

This is a close-up of the many and varied shops that graced Fishergate just a year after the first Preston Guild of the 20th century. G Sutton, Hosier & Glover is first on the left, then the County Hair Dressing Saloons. Lingard Hatter & Outfitter was just by the Preston Gas Company; their two best-selling lines when our photograph was taken were boaters from 1s 6d to 6s 6d and the 'Stanley' top hat, 10s 6d to a guinea. One thing not mentioned is the tunnel that runs under Fishergate. It was built for the tramway which connected the Lancaster Canal with Walton and is now in daily use as an entrance to the Fishergate Centre car park.

FISHERGATE

1903 / 50066

TO · LITERATURE · ARTS · AND · SCIENCES ·

ΑΝΔΡΩΝ ΓΑΡ ΕΠΙΦΑΝΩΝ ΠΑΣΑ ΓΗ ΤΑ

Preston owes a lot to E R Harris, a minister's son who died leaving £300,000 to his native town in 1877. That is the equivalent of about £100,000,000 today. Edmund Robert Harris was the elder son of the Rev R. Harris, Vicar of St George's Church, Preston, for over sixty-four years. His will insisted that the money be used 'to perpetuate the remembrance of his father and his family'; the town not only got a library, but an orphanage, the Harris Institute, and much more. The site for this Library was land given by the Corporation; the foundation stone was laid during Guild Week in 1882 by Lord Lathom.

THE HARRIS PUBLIC LIBRARY AND MUSEUM

1893 / 33087

THE ART GALLERY
AND THE TOWN HALL

1903 / 50084

The Post Office is to the left, the Harris Public Library on the right, and the County Sessions Hall in the middle. There are a few market traders plying their trade, but there are no crowds of customers - it could be early morning before business has got going. After it opened in 1893, the Harris building was just a public library, with a small section of it used as a museum. Two years later the Art Gallery opened, and the whole building came into use.

MARKET SQUARE

1906 / 56123

Here we have Preston's new Post Office, which opened at the turn of the last century. We can see quite clearly the Boer War Memorial at the front of the Post Office. A few years later it was moved to Avenham Park to make way for the Great War Memorial erected to honour those who lost their lives in the First World War which began just twelve months after this photograph was taken. At the time of our photograph, the Post Office opened from 7.30am to 7.30pm six days a week.

THE POST OFFICE

1913 / 65592

THE SESSIONS HOUSE AND THE HARRIS LIBRARY AND ART GALLERY

1913 / 65586

LITERATURE·ARTS·AND·SCIENCES·

27

Preston's War Memorial to those who gave their lives in the Great War had just been erected at this time. The original unveiling date in May 1926 had to be postponed because of the General Strike. There had been a Boer War memorial on this site before this, but it was moved to Avenham Park. You can see it in some of our earlier photographs.

THE WAR MEMORIAL

1926 / 79110

This is a good view of the Great War Memorial which was unveiled in 1926. We can see quite clearly the panel at the front with a helmeted woman holding garlands of victory aloft, with a writhing figure (War) at her feet. To the left we can see down Friargate. The friary of Grey Friars was just to the left of the bottom of the street. Friargate was the second street in Preston to develop shops, and is still a busy shopping area.

THE WAR MEMORIAL AND FRIARGATE

1926 / 79113

FISHERGATE

1929 / 82676

This fine, solid memorial to those who died in the First World War is shown here in close-up. The Memorial was officially unveiled by Earl Jellicoe on 13 June 1926. It was designed by the grandson of Sir Gilbert Scott, who had designed Preston Town Hall. He included a garden area and a surround, seen clearly here, to keep the area slightly cut-off and special.

THE WAR MEMORIAL

1926 / 79115

Here we see the offices and entrance gates of Horrockses, Crewdson & Co on Stanley Street. These gates were built in 1912, the same year that the company was renamed - it was previously John Horrocks'. At the back of this picture are the old works, which date from 1791. John Horrocks was a Preston success, and was always held up as a shining example of man's ingenuity. He arrived in Preston in 1791 from Edgworth, near Bolton. With no real capital, he set to work as a muslin weaver in Turk's Head Court, off Church Street. He put out work for hand-loom weavers, and within a year he had built a factory of his own. Within ten years he had six factories and a house in Golden Square. He had also built Penwortham Lodge, fought a local election, and been elected Member of Parliament. The company he founded became the one we see above.

HORROCKSES, CREWDSON & CO LTD

1913 / 65593

CHURCH STREET

1929 / 82677

Preston was always a town that you had to pass through to go north to south, but as the popularity of Blackpool increased, so did the traffic east to west. Liverpool and Manchester both sent traffic over the Ribble bridges and into the dock area to join roads that were full already. After the First World War, it was decided to build a relief road north of the town: that is what we can see here, just after its completion. Our view shows an almost empty Blackpool Road in the Deepdale area of Preston, Moor Park is on the right. Oh! the hours I have sat in traffic jams on this road in the 1970s and 1980s! To see it new and empty fills me with nostalgia.

NEW ROAD
1924 / 75839

This view shows Penwortham Hill and the climb out of Preston on the Liverpool/Southport road. The newly-erected Penwortham War Memorial is on the right. Note the jaunty open-top car, no doubt heading through Preston and on to Blackpool. There are four modes of transport captured in this photograph - bicycle, horse-drawn carriage, omnibus and car.

PENWORTHAM HILL

1921 / 70736

Here we see the diamond in the crown that is the centre of Preston. After Edmund Harris died in 1877, plans were put in place, for this magnificent public building built in honour of the Harris family. The Harris family provided the money for the building, and Preston Corporation gave the land; work started in 1881. The foundation stone was laid in Guild Week 1882 by Lord Lathom. The Library, designed by Preston architect James Hibbert, was opened on 26 October 1893 by Lord Derby, but it was another two years before the Art Gallery was ready to open. 'To Literature Arts and Sciences' is carved above the classical Greek-style entrance. On the other three sides of the building are carved the following inscriptions: 'The Mental Riches You May Here Acquire, Abide With You Always', 'On Earth There Is Nothing Greater Than Man. In Men There Is Nothing Great But Mind', and 'Reverence In Man, That Which Is Supreme'. These timeless words give food for thought in today's busy world.

THE HARRIS LIBRARY
AND ART GALLERY

1903 / 50083

Designed by H Littler, the County Architect, in 1890 and built in 1900, the County Sessions House stands in Market Square. It was built at a cost of £90,000, which included buying the site. The design is English Renaissance; the tower looks like a wedding cake, with layer on layer climbing 179ft high into the sky. There were two courts when it opened, both furnished in oak, and situated either side of an Assembly Hall. There was also a Grand Jury Room, a Judge's Room, a Solicitors' Room and a Grand Dining Room. Before this was built, the court met at the Old Court House (built in 1827) next to the prison at the bottom of Church Street.

THE COUNTY SESSIONS HOUSE AND WAR MEMORIAL

1926 / 79111

39

THE TOWN HALL

1893 / 33086

Here we see Preston Post Office just a couple of years after it opened. The original Preston Post Office had been at the south end of Wide Shambles in a building leaning on the side of the shambles. When this much-needed new Post Office was built, to make it look more impressive it was faced with stone from Storeton Quarry in the Wirral. After opening, one of its first duties was to produce a special frank for the post, just for the 1902 Guild celebrations. The Post Office was open from 7.30am to 7.30pm most days, and open all day Saturday as well. This photograph it was taken before the Boer War Memorial and Gardens were erected.

THE NEW POST OFFICE

1903 / 50085

THE HARRIS INSTITUTE

1903 / 50071

A workshop for the blind opened in the mid 1850s in a cottage in North Road. In 1866 the Derby School for the Blind was founded, and named in honour of Lord Derby in recognition of his support. In 1893 a site at Fulwood was bought and the fine solid Victorian building we see here was started. The foundation stone was laid on 30 September 1893 by Lady Derby. The school closed in 1987, and the building was turned into offices.

THE HOME FOR THE BLIND

1897 / 40999

The Infirmary was opened in 1870, funded with the money left by Edmund Harris, and in 1884 a Children's Ward had been opened. One of the consultants at the time of our photograph was Sir Charles Brown (1836-1926). Dr Charles Brown was noted for putting his hand in his own pocket if the Hospital had need of any new equipment, especially for the Children's Ward. He was made Medical Officer for Preston in 1870, and in 1905 he paid for a new Operating Theatre to be built at the hospital. This grand gentleman did not retire from service to the Infirmary until 1922, when he was aged 86. As part of Queen Victoria's Diamond Jubilee Honours, the Infirmary was given a royal prefix. It was going to be the Royal Infirmary, Preston, but someone noticed that the initials would have been R I P, so it became Preston Royal Infirmary. The Royal title was removed in 1982, and today it is a hall of residence for students.

THE INFIRMARY
1894 / 34384

The Harris Orphanage opened in 1888 after £100,000 was set aside by the Trustees of the Harris Estate to build and equip such an establishment. Local architect Benjamin Sykes designed the building in domestic Gothic style. At the time of this photograph, there were about one hundred and sixty children resident here. The school was run on the 'group' system (unusual then, and very advanced for the time): the children lived in groups and learnt how to look after one another like a large family. At the age of fifteen the young adults were launched into the real world, or returned to any relatives that could be found. The Orphanage had a gymnasium, swimming baths, a hospital, workshops and a chapel, so every care was given to its charges. In 1914 Clayton Hall was built in the grounds to give added leisure facilities; it cost £2,000. In 1948 the building became Fulwood and Caldy Comprehensive School, which later merged with Ingol and Lightfoot Primary School to become the Harris County Primary School.

THE HARRIS ORPHANAGE

1893 / 33098

The foundation stone of the Victoria Jubilee Technical School was laid in July 1895; the purpose of the School was to give relief to the over-full Harris Institute. The School was declared open by the Countess of Derby in September 1897, and was an immediate success. Many of the classes and facilities were connected to local industries, and there was a whole department for training for the cotton industry. There was a warping and winding room, and a weaving shed with eighty hand looms and twenty power looms. The school developed facilities for teaching electrical skills, and an Electrical Engineering Laboratory was added in Edwardian times. The building has been added to and rebuilt, and is now part of the University of Central Lancashire.

THE TECHNICAL SCHOOL

1903 / 50070

Preston was a County Borough until 1974. County Hall was built in 1882 and was the administrative headquarters of Lancashire County Council. The County Magistrates' Court ran on simple and firm sets of rules, relying on moral and ethical principles as much as on legislature. Because of the work of the county council the building soon became too small, and in 1930 the council were occupying no less than seven other buildings. A further block was built in 1934 (at a cost of £130,000) on Pitt Street and Marchand Street.

COUNTY HALL

1894 / 34385

THE PARISH CHURCH

1893 / 33088

This unusual view of Preston Parish Church was taken from the back of the church. There has been a church on this site since the 7th century; the first church was dedicated to St Wilfrid. Later on, when the Guilds were established, the dedication was changed to St John the Divine, who was patron saint of the Guild Merchants. The church was rebuilt in 1770 and 1854. In 1855 it was altered and restored at a cost of £9,500, and a further £2,000 was spent in 1885 to improve the church and put in gas fittings. When you enter the church today, you cannot help being impressed with the strong military connections displayed - there are many army memorials to be seen.

ST WALBURGE'S CHURCH

1897 / 40996

This photograph of the docks was taken just a year after they were opened. Here we see the Albert Edward Dock basin, looking from the entrance towards the town. Amongst the cargo which was being unloaded here in our picture would have been timber, flax and china clay.

THE DOCKS

1893 / 33097

It was this river bank area that had been used as berthing places for small ships carrying flax, which came to the town long before the docks were opened. As we can see, when the tide went out and the river was low nothing much could go on, though some ships could continue to unload once they were tied up. On the skyline you can see the bulk of one of the dock buildings, and the impressive spire of St Walburge's Church.

THE RIBBLE
1926 / 79117

Although they are referred to as docks, there was really only one dock, the Albert Edward Dock. It was named in honour of Queen Victoria's second son, who opened the dock when he was the Duke of Edinburgh. At the time of our picture, vessels of up to 51,000 tons could use the dock, and there was a 21ft draught. Petroleum products were among the imports, as were bananas. The ship in the centre is the 'Canford', registered in London, with a Bremen ship in the right-hand corner.

THE DOCKS

C1955 / P113033

Timber had always been one of Preston's main imports. Even before the docks opened, timber-carrying ships from all over Europe would come into these sheltered waters near Penwortham Hill and unload. Just before the First World War, the port went through a very bad patch owing to shifting sands at the river mouth. The year 1909 saw hardly any but the smallest boats in Preston Docks, and the council had to dig deep into their coffers for dredging work before things started to pick up again.

THE TIMBER QUAY

NORTH SIDE c1955 / P113047

We can see two of the four tugs that the corporation, who ran the docks, had bought. Three were named after councillors who had supported the movement to build the docks: they were the 'Charles Hearn', the 'John Herbert' and the 'Frank Jamieson', and the fourth was the 'Hewitt'. The docks had an area of 850ft by 300ft, equalling forty acres of water. There was also a dock basin at the river entrance of four and half acres of water. In the fifties there was a weekly delivery of bananas from the Windward and Leeward Islands, and a ripening shed had to be built on the docks.

THE DOCKS

EAST SIDE c1955 / P113045

In this photograph we can see wood stacked for seasoning within the dock area. Frequent visitors here were the Russian ships bringing in hardwoods. In October 1964 the Russian MV 'Igarkales' caught fire while it was still half unloaded. Firefighting was hampered by the fact that the crew spoke no English, and could not be understood when they raised the alarm. Owing to the Cold War, the Russian captain was under orders not to let anyone British on board, which made matters even worse. Union troubles did not help the port, which in all honesty was never a great success - at best it broke even. In the 1960s weekly freight services to Ireland were launched, sailing to Londonderry, Portrush, Dublin and Waterford, and the port was amongst the first to offer a roll-on, roll-off service for taking vehicles over to Ireland.

THE DOCKS
NORTH SIDE c1960 / P113049

The fight to save the docks was a long and bitter battle. The council had been losing money for year on year, and felt that the drain on council rates was not good for the town. There were so many other uses for the money which was being used to prop up the ailing docks. Yet they did provide work for local people: at the time of our photograph around 500 worked there, and many more provided ancillary services. By October 1981 the council were deep in talks to re-develop the dock area. Today this area is offices and supermarkets, and the re-development is thought to be a success.

THE DOCKS
NORTH SIDE c1960 / P113050

Having Avenham Park in the background does enhance the pleasure of a walk over the bridge. Avenham Tower can be seen in the trees to the right, and the paths lead away to Frenchwood. The bridge was designed by William Cartwright, the canal's civil engineer, who was also an optician in Preston and an inventor of some note. In 1936 the swollen river flooded some allotments and washed away a hen shed, which hit the bridge. Without much debate the broken bridge was repaired, and the citizens continued to enjoy their promenades. Some early postcards refer to the Walk as 'Lovers' Lane'.

THE TRAM BRIDGE

1903 / 50073

THE TRAM BRIDGE

c1955 / P113007

The bridge started to show its age soon after our photograph was taken, and by the mid 1960s it was declared unsafe. Again it could have been pulled down, but it was saved and rebuilt to the original design in concrete. It is now the only footbridge over the River Ribble here, and a great asset to the parks and recreation facilities of Preston.

Here we see the river bank of the Ribble just west of the main railway bridge at the end of South Meadows. The dray on the left is delivering to the Pleasure Boat Inn, which is hidden by trees on the left of the picture. The landlord hired out boats by the hour, as well as providing trips up and down the river. He had the unfortunate name of Mr Crook. The railway bridge here was built in 1838 by North Union Railways for the Preston to Wigan line at a cost of £70,000, and is now part of the west coast main line.

THE BRIDGE OVER THE RIBBLE

1903 / 50077

This wonderful nostalgic photograph shows steam engine 'black 5', the
work-horse of the LMS region, heading south with non-corridor stock
on a local, probably to Bamber Bridge and on to Blackburn. The three
young lads out in a rowing boat sum up the simple pleasures of the mid
1950s, the quiet void before the rock 'n roll era and the Swinging 60s
began. Today, it is quite hard to get down to the river in some places, but
the Ribble is still there waiting to be reinvented.

THE RIVER RIBBLE FROM MILLER PARK

C1955 / P113018

Still the main street of Preston, Fishergate shows off some of its very varied shops. The spire of the parish church dominates the centre of the photograph. Corporation buses - how fondly they are remembered today! They were on time, they had a conductor to help and take fares, and the prices never seemed to change. On the left of the picture just behind the lamp post you can just make out the remains of Preston Town Hall, which had burnt down in 1947. These remains stayed there until October 1961, when a clearing-away programme began.

FISHERGATE

c1955 / P113026

The Institute for the Diffusion of Useful Knowledge has stood up well to the passing of time. At this point it is the Art College, and the rock-pop era is about to break in on our rather sedate photograph. The duffle-coats and beat-niks, the anti-war protests and folk clubs that started then are just a year or so away, and now only a memory.

THE HARRIS INSTITUTE

C1955 / P113017

Preston also had a covered market, so this busy scene could be the yearly Pot Market, which took place in the square for eight days every August. Traditionally it was a noisy fair, with the stall-holders allowed to shout to advertise their wares. Two centuries ago, Preston had a market every Saturday at first light, then a linen market, and then when everything was sold, a fish market and a cattle market.

THE MARKET PLACE

C1955 / P113015

This view shows the August Pot Market. Locals refer to this area as the 'Flag Market'. On the left of the picture you can see some of the locals listening to the patter of an auctioneer telling them of all the wonderful bargains he was about to let them have. The squarish carts were used to carry the pottery to and from the markets. A local delicacy sold from stalls around the market was black-eyed peas with vinegar or mint sauce, and new potatoes dripping in best butter with mint sauce. Lovely!

THE MARKET SQUARE

C1955 / P113014

An unusual view that can only have been taken from the remains of Preston Town Hall. The Flag Market area lies below our photographer, and Cheapside runs at the bottom left-hand corner. Friargate is the street running off to the left, and Market Street runs alongside the Post Office, which is just caught on the right of the picture. Parking in Market Square is a luxury which we have not been allowed for many years now.

FRIARGATE

C1955 / P113022

Friargate was still full of traffic at this time, and not the pedestrianised area it is today. The friary that gave its name to the street was founded in the early 13th century by the Franciscan order of Grey Friars; they also founded the Leper Hospital of St Mary Magdalen, and Magdalen Land became Maud Land.

THE POST OFFICE AND
THE WAR MEMORIAL

c1960 / P113076

The Main General Post Office is on the left of the photograph. Gone are the days when it opened seven days a week from 7.30am to late in the evening. At the time of this photograph, the Post Office had announced the Saturday afternoon closing of the smaller offices and the cut-back of Sunday services in an effort to make more profit.

THE APPROACHES
TO THE COVERED MARKET

c1960 / P113076

This market was locally called the Covered Market. Plans were put in hand as early as 1868 to build a Market Hall on this site, which was previously known as the Orchard. On 6 August 1870 the roof of the market fell in while it was being constructed, and after an enquiry the work was passed to a local shipbuilder, William Allsup. He decided not to put sides on the structure, and it was completed and finally opened in 1875. A new wholesale fruit and vegetable market opened in 1967.

THE MARKET

c1960 / P113073

There are bargains galore in the Covered Market. Our photograph does demonstrate just how open you were to the wind and rain, especially on the outside parts of the market. A hundred years earlier than our photograph, there would have been four cattle markets every week. Store cattle were sold on Monday, fat stock on Tuesday, store pigs on Wednesday and on Friday it was dairy cattle. Many of the animals were brought down the Lancashire Canal and held at the loading dock in the Marsh Lane/Corporation Street area.

THE MARKET
C1960 / P113075

This view looks from Market Square down Friargate. The Maypole Grocery Store (dried peas 1s 6d), Boots the Chemist and Halfords (everything for your Raleigh bicycle) are the shops overlooking the War Memorial, which by then had had the names added of the fallen of the Second World War.

THE POST OFFICE
AND THE MEMORIAL

c1965 / P113077

Here we have a good view of the area that is to the west of Market Square. Stylo Shoe Shop, John Collier ('the window to watch'), Richard Shops and Stead & Simpson are among the many varied shops facing the Market. It is nostalgic to see the cars parked in the street - the Morris Minor and mini-vans for example - and no yellow lines and no parking meters. Those were halcyon days.

CHEAPSIDE

c1960 / P113079

We are looking down towards the railway station in the distance; on the right is Cheapside, and Glover's Court is to the left. There are no traffic lights at this busy junction, so a policeman on his wood and canvas podium directs the traffic. Again we get a good idea of the diversity of shops in Preston, including Jackson's the Tailors, Redmans, 'the Good Bacon Shop', and many more that pulled in the shoppers from miles around the town.

FISHERGATE

c1965 / P113080

THE AVENHAM COLONNADE

1893 / 33090

*With its double row of lime trees and its scenic views over the River Ribble,
Avenham Walk has always been popular. It was marked out officially as
early as 1728, though it is thought that it had been in use from 1696.
Lime trees were chosen because they grow slowly; some of those in this
picture are still there today.*

This photograph, showing the pond, looks over what was known as the Valley. Both Avenham and Miller Park were started around 1864. As well as being lovely parks for the people, they were begun to provide work for some of the thousands laid off due to the cotton famine, which was caused by the American Civil War. The two parks are divided by a railway embankment that was already there.

AVENHAM PARK

1903 / 50087

The land for the park was given by Lt Col Cross, who lived in a large and impressive house at the Red Scar. The council bought the strip of land alongside the railway, and the area was ready to be developed. Before the Second World War, if the weather was very cold, the Fire Department would flood to a couple of inches the area between the Rockery and the Bandstand that you can see in this photograph, and people would come and ice-skate there.

THE ROCK GARDENS AND LAWNS

AVENHAM PARK c1955 / P113011

AVENHAM PARK

THE FORTY STEPS   1924 / 75842

This is a view that Edward Geoffrey Stanley's statue enjoyed from the Derby Terrace. The bridge is the railway bridge over the River Ribble, and we can see the far bank clearly. Nearer to the camera is the fountain with four figures round the base that represent Earth, Air, Water and Fire, and we can see some of the classic urns which graced the steps and surrounds.

MILLER PARK

1893 / 33092

This view shows the Derby Terrace and its visitors. The Earl's statue was placed here after he donated over £5,000 to the Relief Fund to help the starving of Lancashire during the 1860s cotton famine. He had at one time been MP for Preston, but was MP for North Lancashire at the time. The pedestal is 15ft high and made of Aberdeen granite, and the statue is 11ft high and carved from Sicilian marble. The cost was £2,500, and £349 of that was raised by a penny subscription by workmen. In 1912, suffragettes led by a Preston woman, Edith Rigby, tarred and feathered the statue after the 16th Earl (son of our statue) strongly opposed votes for women. Though the statue was cleaned, you can still see traces of the incident.

MILLER PARK

1913 / 65597

This is a good overall view of the statue of Lord Derby in its magnificent setting, with the Park Hotel behind. The hotel was always slow to modernise, and at the time of this picture it had no bar (was this owing to the T-Total movement in Preston, I wonder?). If guests wanted a drink, they had to have it specially taken to their rooms. Until 1932 hot running water was not available, and anyone wanting a bath would have to telephone down, and again the hot water had to be brought specially to the room. Only the ground floor had central heating, while all the other floors had to rely on coal fires. British Rail sold the building to the County Council in 1950; it was re-vamped, and is now the East Cliff County Offices occupied by the Regional Health Authority.

MILLER PARK

1925 / 77922

Moor Park is actually Preston's oldest open space. At one time any Guild Freeman was allowed to graze cattle here at no charge. The corporation took that right away when they enclosed the area in 1834, and plans for a park were first mentioned a few years later. By 1836 the lake, the Serpentine, had been built, and so had three lodges. It cost £11,000 to drain and level Moor Park and make roads and paths.

MOOR PARK
1913 / 65596

Moor Park was always a popular place for children, and I bet our young ladies in the picture had had a smashing time. There was at this time a set of swings for girls and another set for boys, and the playground was also divided. Moor Park had an open-air swimming pool as well. The pool was opened on 7 June 1907 by Alderman Woods. The 32yds by 16yds pool, only 3ft to 4ft 6ins deep, was very popular with the children. It lasted until the early 1970s.

MOOR PARK

1924 / 75840

MOOR PARK AVENUE

1903 / 50088

Moor Park, the largest of Preston's parks at 110 acres, lies a mile to the north of the town centre. Here we see the Park's main entrance. Like Preston's two other parks, it was created to provide work for the unemployed, and like Miller and Avenham Parks it was laid out and designed by the London landscape gardener Edward Milner. It was begun in 1864 and opened on 4 October 1867, just one day after the other two parks.

Broughton is on the Great North Road (the A6), and has managed not to be swallowed up by Preston. Here we see the ancient parish church of St John the Baptist. It is only the tower of this church that is ancient; it dates from the 16th century. Broughton means 'the place by the brook'. The brook that gave it its name was Woodplumpton Brook, which runs past Broughton House.

BROUGHTON
THE CHURCH
c1955 / B718001

The High Street may look quiet and rural, but five years earlier this street was pounded with traffic day and night. The cars parked on the pavement gives a hint of the traffic problems caused by people heading to the Lakes or southwards. In the summer time and on Bank Holidays, you could be an hour just getting through this mile-long village. The Preston by-pass opened in 1959, and the motorway from junction 32 near Broughton to junction 33 at Hampson Green opened six years later. That gave the villagers a little of their peace back.

BROUGHTON
THE HIGH STREET C1965 / B718010

BALDERSTONE

ST LEONARD'S CHURCH c1955 / B852011

This is another view of Stanifield Lane, but further out from the village. The pre-war houses stand neat and square on the lane. Farington is a parish in South Ribble Borough.

FARINGTON

STANIFIELD LANE c1955 / F223003

Stanifield Lane is one of the two main roads that go through Farington, which is south of Preston and roughly half-way to Leyland. This photograph reflects the innocence and simplicity of the 1950s: note the gate post with an advertisement painted on it, the motor bike and sidecar, bikes with shopping baskets and the lady with rollers and scarf just nipping out to the corner shop.

FARINGTON
STANIFIELD LANE c1955 / F223006

Fulwood is north of Preston, sitting astride the A6, the Great North Road. It was an Urban District in its own right. Our photograph of Beech Drive shows how the area was, mainly residential. At the time of this photograph there were more than 18,000 people living in the 33,164 acres - 2,400 houses were built here between 1945 and 1965. This area was the site of part of the Battle of Ribbleton Moor, and cannon balls and bones were found here more than once while all that building was going on.

FULWOOD

BEECH DRIVE c1965 / F198015

The name Fulwood comes from the Old English and means 'dirty or foul wood'. Here we see the main road leading north from Preston and the Methodist Church. The Harris Orphanage was built out here in 1888 so that the children could benefit from the fresh country air away from the grimy town.

FULWOOD

THE METHODIST CHURCH   c1965 / F198002

Longridge stands about six miles from Preston on the Clitheroe Road. It still shows many of the signs of a country village, and is complete with its Market Square, as our photograph shows. Longridge takes its name from being at the end of Longridge Fell. The Dog Inn is on the right, and Sanderson the Butcher is across the road on the corner.

LONGRIDGE

MARKET PLACE C1955 / L340006

LONGRIDGE

LITTLE LANE c1955 / L340014

Here we see a quiet rural scene in a typical Lancashire village. The village had three churches at the time, and two unusual wayside monuments.

LONGRIDGE

BERRY LANE c1955 / L340004

We are looking down Berry Lane back towards Preston. Longridge was an Urban District Council; it comprised 3,285 acres, and when this photograph was taken had around 5,320 people living in the area, which included Alston and Dilworth.

LONGRIDGE

BERRY LANE c1955 / L340012

This view shows the level crossing at the bottom of Berry Lane. There is a National Coal Board Depot on the left, and just above the sign we can see the tower of the parish church, St Lawrence's. The tower was built in 1841. Many of the shops have their blinds out, so it cannot be a Wednesday - that was half-day closing.

We are looking towards the centre of Mellor Brook. The Feilden's Arms, seen at the top of the hill in the photograph at the bottom of the previous page is on the left. As we can see from the advertisements on the wall, it sold C & S Blackpool Ales, and the landlord was Mr J Kay; he also sold teas, snacks and ices.

MELLOR BROOK
THE VILLAGE c1955 / M309001

This is the A49, and we can see the Feilden's Arms head on. Because Samlesbury Hall was so near, the area was popular with walkers and day trippers in the post-war years. You can see the local post office on the left of the road with a telephone box outside.

MELLOR BROOK

THE POST OFFICE c1955 / M309010

PENWORTHAM

THE CHURCH AND THE LYCH GATE 1903 / 50075

Here we have a lovely view of St Mary's, the parish church of Penwortham. The most famous person resting here must be John Horrocks, who founded his great cotton empire at Preston. You can see the iron railings around his grave at the bottom left of our picture. The church is built in Perpendicular style.

PENWORTHAM
THE CHURCH 1893 / 33102

The Old Unicorn Inn lies at the centre of Walton-le-Dale. The inn also had a dining room and tea rooms. It was in this area in 1648 that Cromwell made his headquarters, and he is reputed to have stayed at the Old Unicorn.

WALTON-LE-DALE

THE OLD UNICORN, CHORLEY ROAD c1955 / W524002

This parish church, situated in Cuerdale Lane, is more or less unchanged since the 17th century. In Roman times, Walton-le-Dale was known as Rigodunum, and in Saxon times it was called Waelletune. The manor was granted to Robert Bannastre by Henry de Lacy in the 12th century.

WALTON-LE-DALE

ST LEONARD'S CHURCH C1955 / W524006

This view shows the main road through Walton-le-Dale. Walton-le-Dale Urban District included Higher Walton, Gregson Lane, Bamber Bridge and Lostock Hall as well as Walton itself. Victoria Road was part of the A6; it was constructed along the line of the old Roman Road that went through here.

WALTON-LE-DALE
VICTORIA ROAD C1955 / W524005

Whalley is a very ancient town and steeped in history. The Abbey was begun in the 12th century, and its ruins (seen here ivy-covered, as they used to be) have been a place to visit for over three hundred years. The church at Whalley is equally interesting, and it has a St Cuthbert Cross in the churchyard.

WHALLEY

THE ABBEY CLOISTER 1894 / 34332

The driveway up to the Tower is as long and straight as a Roman road. Built by the de Hoghton family at the time of Queen Elizabeth I, the tower is built around two courtyards. The house is historically very interesting, and there are many mysterious tales about it.

HOGHTON TOWER

1895 / 35719

This unusual view of Stoneyhurst College shows the chapel on the left. There are many articles of interest from the past kept at the school, including Mary Queen of Scots' book of hours and Bonny Prince Charlie's flask. The College is open to visitors every summer, and is well worth the effort to see.

STONEYHURST
THE COLLEGE 1899 / 43487

Here we see the back of the college. The Shireburn family lie in the ancient church of Mitton just a few miles away from the College. The Shireburn family's daughter married the Duke of Norfolk; she returned to give her family members buried in the chapel grand memorials.

STONEYHURST
THE COLLEGE 1893 / 33105

Built as Stoneyhurst Hall by Sir Richard Shireburn, the building was abandoned by the family and given to the Catholic Church; it became a school run by Jesuit Priests. Stoneyhurst College had a reputation which spread all over the world, and its former pupils included the actor Charles Laughton and Conan Doyle, the creator of Sherlock Holmes.

STONEYHURST

THE COLLEGE FROM THE WEST   1893 / 33104

INDEX

PLEASE HELP US BRING FRITH'S PHOTOGRAPHS TO LIFE

Our authors do their best to recount the history of the places they write about. They give insights into how particular towns and villages developed, they describe the architecture of streets and buildings, and they discuss the lives of famous people who lived there. But however knowledgeable our authors are, the story they tell is necessarily incomplete.

Frith's photographs are so much more than plain historical documents. They are living proofs of the flow of human life down the generations. They show real people at real moments in history; and each of those people is the son or daughter of someone, the brother or sister, aunt or uncle, grandfather or grandmother of someone else. All of them lived, worked and played in the streets depicted in Frith's photographs.

We would be grateful if you would tell us about the many places shown in our photographs—the streets with their buildings, shops, businesses and industries. Describe your own memories of life in those streets: what it was like growing up there, who ran the local shop and what shopping was like years ago; if your workplace is shown tell us about your working day and what the building is used for now. With your help more and more Frith photographs can be brought to life, and vital memories preserved for posterity.

We will gradually add your comments and stories to the archive for the benefit of historians of the future. Wherever possible, we will try to include some of your comments in future editions of our books. Moreover, if you spot errors in dates, titles or other facts, please let us know, because our archive records are not always completely accurate—they rely on 150 years of human endeavour and hand-compiled records.

So please write, fax or email us with your stories and memories. Thank you!

FREE PRINT OF YOUR CHOICE

Choose any Frith photograph in this book.
Simply complete the Voucher opposite and
return it with your remittance for £2.25 (to
cover postage and handling) and we will print
the photograph of your choice in SEPIA (size
11 x 8 inches) and supply it in a cream mount
with a burgundy rule line
(overall size 14 x 11 inches).
**Please note: photographs with a reference number
starting with a "Z" are not Frith photographs and
cannot be supplied under this offer.**
Offer valid for delivery to UK one address only.

Mounted Print
Overall size 14 x 11 inches (355 x 280mm)

PLUS: **Order additional Mounted Prints at
HALF PRICE - £7.49 each** (normally £14.99)
If you would like to order more Frith prints
from this book, possibly as gifts for friends and
family, you can buy them at half price (with no
additional postage and handling costs).

PLUS: **Have your Mounted Prints framed**
For an extra £14.95 per print you can have your
mounted print(s) framed in an elegant polished
wood and gilt moulding, overall size
16 x 13 inches (no additional postage and
handling required).

IMPORTANT!

These special prices are only
available if you use this form to
order. You must use the ORIGINAL
VOUCHER (no copies permitted).

We can only despatch to one
UK address. This offer cannot be
combined with any other offer.

FRITH PRODUCTS AND SERVICES

All Frith photographs are available for you to buy as framed or mounted prints.
From time to time, other illustrated items such as Address Books and Maps are also
available. Already, almost 80,000 Frith archive photographs can be viewed and
purchased on the internet through the Frith website.

For more detailed information on Frith companies and products, visit:

www.francisfrith.co.uk

For further information, or trade enquiries, contact:

The Francis Frith Collection, Frith's Barn, Teffont, Salisbury SP3 5QP

Tel: +44 (0) 1722 716 376 Fax: +44 (0) 1722 716 881 Email: sales@francisfrith.co.uk

Voucher

for FREE
and Reduced Price
Frith Prints

*Do not photocopy this voucher. Only the original is valid, so please fill it in,
cut it out and return it to us with your order.*

	Picture ref no	Page number	Qty	Mounted @ £7.49	Framed + £14.95	Orders Total £
1			1	Free of charge*	£	£
2				£7.49	£	£
3				£7.49	£	£
4				£7.49	£	£
5				£7.49	£	£
6				£7.49	£	£
Please allow 28 days for delivery. Offer available to one UK address only				* Post & handling		£2.25
				Total Order Cost		£

Title of this book . . . .

I enclose a cheque / postal order for £ . . . .
payable to 'The Francis Frith Collection'

OR debit my Mastercard / Visa / Maestro / Amex card

Card Number

Issue No (Maestro only)   Valid from (Amex/Maestro)

Expires   Signature

Name Mr/Mrs/Ms . . . .

Address . . . .

. . . .

. . . .

. . . . .Postcode. . . . .

Daytime Tel No . . . .

E-mail . . . .

Valid to 31/12/07